SPECIAL EDUCATIONAL NEEDS

POLICY OPTIONS STEERING GROUP

POLICY PAPER 3
(third series)

Early Years Development and Special Educational Needs

A NASEN PUBLICATION

Published in 2000

© NASEN

All rights reserved. No part of this publication may be reproduced or transmitted in any form or by any means, electronic, mechanical, photocopying, recording, or otherwise without the prior permission of the publishers.

ISBN 1 901485 21 8

Published by NASEN.
NASEN is a company limited by guarantee, registered in England and Wales. Company No. 2674379.
NASEN is a registered charity. Charity No. 1007023.

Further copies of this book and details of NASEN's many other publications may be obtained from the Publications Department at its registered office:
NASEN House, 4/5, Amber Business Village, Amber Close, Amington, Tamworth, Staffs. B77 4RP.
Tel: 01827 311500; Fax: 01827 313005
Email: welcome@nasen.org.uk
Web site: www.nasen.org.uk

Cover design by Tableau Reproductions.
Typeset in Times by J. C. Typesetting and printed in the United Kingdom by Stowes (Stoke-on-Trent).

Special Educational Needs Policy Options Steering Group

Early Years Development and Special Educational Needs

POLICY PAPER 3
(third series)

Edited by Brahm Norwich

Contents

	Page
1. Introduction to Policy Paper	5
2. Special Needs in the Early Years: Policy Options and Practice Prospects Sheila Wolfendale	9
3. Developing a Comprehensive and Integrated Approach to Early Years Services for Children with Special Educational Needs - Opportunities and Challenges in Current Government Initiatives Philippa Russell	23
4. Summary of Discussion Brahm Norwich and Geoff Lindsay	42

Chapter 1
Introduction to Policy Paper

This paper is a record of the recent invited Policy Seminar held at the Institute of Education, London University (9 December 1999) which examined the question of early years development and special educational needs in the third round of these SEN Policy Option Seminar series. The aim of the seminar was to consider SEN issues and perspectives on the early years, especially in the context of recent developments in the field. This was the first time that the Policy Options series had focused on this topic. It was an important one in view of the emphasis placed on early intervention in education and wider social policy.

The main papers were presented by two very well known people in the field: Professor Sheila Wolfendale, an Educational Psychologist from the Department of Psychology, University of East London; and Philippa Russell for the Council for Disabled Children. In addition to the main papers there is a brief summary of the general discussion. About 45 people participated in the day seminar, coming from schools, LEA support services, LEA officers, DfEE, Government agencies, parent groups, the voluntary sector, health service professionals, educational psychologists and universities.

SEN Policy Options Steering Group
Background

This policy paper is the third in the third series of seminars and conferences to be organised by the SEN Policy Options Steering Group. This group organised the initial ESRC-Cadbury Trust series on policy options for special educational needs in the 1990s. The success of the first series led to the second one which was supported financially by NASEN. (See the list of these policy papers published by NASEN at the end of this section.) The Steering Group has representatives from LEA administrators, head teachers, voluntary organisations, professional associations, universities and research. The further success of the second series of policy seminars and papers led to this round of seminars which has also been organised with further funding from NASEN. These events are intended to consider current and future policy issues in the field in a proactive way. They are planned to interest all those concerned with policy matters in special educational needs.

Aims and objectives of the Policy Options Group

1. to identify current and likely future policy problems and the options for solutions in special education provision following the Green Paper 1997 through to the year 2000 and beyond;

2. to organise conferences and seminars for policy-makers, professionals, parents, voluntary associations and researchers in the field and publish the proceedings for wider dissemination;

3. to enhance the two-way relationship between policy and service issues and research agendas.

Current Steering Group membership

Mr Keith Bovair, Head teacher Durrants School (NASEN representative); Mr Clive Danks, Advisor, Birmingham LEA; Mr Tony Dessent, Director of Education, Luton LEA; Mr Peter Gray, SEN Policy Consultant; Dr Seamus Hegarty, Director of the National Foundation for Educational Research; Professor Geoff Lindsay, Warwick University; Dr Ingrid Lunt, Reader, Institute of Education, London University; Mr Vincent McDonnell, Director of Education, Islington LEA; Mr Chris Marshall (OFSTED); Professor Brahm Norwich, School of Education, Exeter University; Mrs Margaret Peter; Mrs Philippa Russell, Director of Council for Disabled Children; Professor Klaus Wedell, Institute of Education, London University.

Current series

The current series aims to organise four full or half-day events on special education policy and provision over two years which are relevant to the context of considerable changes in the education system.

If you have any ideas about possible topics or would like to know more about the events, please do contact a member of the Group or Brahm Norwich at the School of Education, University of Exeter, Heavitree Road, Exeter EX1 2LU (email b.norwich@exeter.ac.uk).

Policy Options Papers from first seminar series published and available from NASEN

1. Bucking the Market: LEAs and Special Needs
Peter Housden, Chief Education Officer, Nottinghamshire LEA.

2. **Towards Effective Schools for All**
   Mel Ainscow, Cambridge University Institute of Education.

3. **Teacher Education for Special Educational Needs**
   Professor Peter Mittler, Manchester University.

4. **Allocating Resources for SEN Provision**
   Jennifer Evans and Ingrid Lunt, Institute of Education, London University.

5. **Planning and Diversity: Special Schools and Their Alternatives**
   Max Hunt, Director of Education, Stockport LEA.

6. **Options for Partnership between Health, Education and Social Services**
   Tony Dessent, Senior Assistant Director, Nottinghamshire LEA.

7. **Provision for Special Educational Needs from the Perspectives of Service Users**
   Micheline Mason, Robina Mallet, Colin Low and Philippa Russell.

Policy Options Papers from second seminar series published and available from NASEN

1. **Independence and Interdependence? Responsibilities for SEN in the Unitary and County Authorities**
   Roy Atkinson, Michael Peters, Derek Jones, Simon Gardner and Philippa Russell.

2. **Inclusion or Exclusion: Future Policy for Emotional and Behavioural Difficulties**
   John Bangs, Peter Gray and Greg Richardson.

3. **Baseline Assessment: Benefits and Pitfalls**
   Geoff Lindsay, Max Hunt, Sheila Wolfendale, Peter Tymms.

4. **Future Policy for SEN: Responding to the Green Paper**
   Brahm Norwich, Ann Lewis, John Moore, Harry Daniels.

Policy Options Papers from third seminar series published and available from NASEN

1. **Rethinking Support for More Inclusive Schooling**
   Peter Gray, Clive Danks, Rik Boxer, Barbara Burke, Jeff Frank, Ruth Newbury, Joan Baxter.

2. **Developments in Additional Resource Allocation to Promote Greater Inclusion**
   John Moore, Cor Meijer, Klaus Wedell, Paul Croll and Diana Moses.

Chapter 2
Special Needs in the Early Years:
Policy Options and Practice Prospects

SHEILA WOLFENDALE, Psychology Department,
University of East London

Introduction

I welcome this opportunity to scrutinise an area of special educational needs (SEN) that has, in some demonstrable ways, and at some times, been neglected or marginalised.

The raison d'être of Policy Options seminars and ensuing publications is to look prospectively and gauge emerging policy and practice for the near and middle future.

I certainly plan to do that, but because I perceive that a number of gaps and deficits in early years (EY) and special needs have hindered policy and practice development, I propose to address these, too. One of my aims is to attempt to reposition SEN within the early years, so that its place is secure within an inclusive framework.

Potentially the field is vast; early years development and childcare provision cross agency lines and no one agency currently has a monopoly in this area. Furthermore, differential legislation covering, variously, 'need' and 'special educational needs' (viz. *1989 Children Act*, and *1981/1993/1996 Education Acts*) may not have facilitated a unified approach to SEN in the early years. There are signs that more recent legislation (especially see the *School Standards and Frameworks Act 1998*, and Early Years Development Plans) and Government intentions (e.g. to rationalise the present disparate systems of inspecting early years provision by unifying these into a single system under the control and jurisdiction of OFSTED) in addition to the SEN programme of action will serve to place SEN firmly in all early years trans-disciplinary endeavours (see Roffey 1999, page 14, for a useful legislative summary).

My intention is to offer a number of propositions and briefly comment on each of these. The purpose of this is to (a) identify areas of disparity and gaps in the EY and SEN realms, (b) indicate where progress has been sluggish, (c) point to encouraging signs regarding improved provision and co-ordination and attitude change. I will then select a number of key policy and practice areas for discussion.

PROPOSITION 1: That historically and until very recently few LEAs have had an early years policy that has jointly encompassed the early years and SEN domains.

Comments

- Evidence for this proposition comes from the availability of a number of otherwise impressive LEA EY policy documents/practice manuals in which reference to special needs is brief and incidental. Many practitioners who have a solid early years experience base do not have commensurate SEN experience. How could they? Even cross-reference to the SEN *Code of Practice* may be superficial.

- With the advent of and requirement for SEN (how SEN will be met, etc.) within Early Years Partnership Plans, the portents are positive that such omissions will be redressed. Also, criteria for the designation of Early Excellence Centres (an innovation of the current Government) include the ability of such establishments to meet special needs.

- New OFSTED inspection arrangements will, I am sure, ensure that special needs provision will be inspected using consistent criteria across all types of establishments. It is to be hoped that Portage Services inspection, currently the domain of Social Services, will also be incorporated into a new unified inspection system.

PROPOSITION 2: *That traditionally, LEA SEN policies likewise, as above, have not acknowledged or referred to (their) LEA Early Years policies.*

Comments

- Evidence suggests that, post-1993 Education Act and following the *Code of Practice*, LEA SEN Handbooks and Manuals do not, typically, contextualise EY/SEN within the wider EY policy domain.

- The section on Under Fives in the 1994 SEN *Code of Practice* contains a section on 'Moving to Primary School' (5.28 pp. 104-105) which only in a limited way contextualises broader Reception/Year 1 curriculum opportunities.

- We can confidently anticipate that the revised *Code of Practice* will contain cross-reference to Baseline Assessment requirements (NASEN Policy Paper 3, 1998) and perhaps, too, to the QCA Early Learning Goals (1999 and see below).

***PROPOSITION 3:** That, at national level, there has been an historical separation of powers, interests and responsibilities in the areas of early years and SEN.*

Comments

- The major national early years forum, The Early Childhood Education Forum, is an impressive and influential coalition of around 35 mostly early years organisations. However, special needs is under-represented, with only four bodies which can be said to represent broad SEN issues (the National Portage Association, MENCAP, the Council for Disabled Children, the Association of Educational Psychologists, but not NASEN).

- Several notable reports into early years provision in the last decade (e.g. Rumbold Report 1990, to name but one) refer to preschoolers with special needs en passant.

- Likewise, the Desirable Learning Outcomes (SCAA/QCA), the precursor to the Early Learning Goals (1999, and see below), cross-referred only superficially to the identification of and differential curriculum for young children with possible special needs.

- Such marginalised treatment of SEN in the early years is also reflected in an OFSTED Report reviewing the quality of nursery education (OFSTED, 1999) which does not discuss progress made by selected, visited early years establishments in meeting SEN, but does, *specifically*, in the same document report upon 25 Portage Services (incidentally very positively).

- Encouraging signs at national level pointing to (a) realignment of general early years and SEN, (b) bringing SEN in the early years into a more central position including pronouncements and promises contained in the DfEE *Programme of Action* (1998a) and a number of major intervention initiatives targeted at early years (and beyond) such as SURE START (Glass, 1999), Family Literacy, via, e.g. BOOK-START (Wade and Moore, 2000, in press) and *Parenting Education and Support Programmes* (Wolfendale and Einzig, 1999).

In general, however, and notwithstanding the dissonance and discrepancies reported above, post-*1981 Education Act*, the profile of special needs in the early years has risen (Wolfendale & Wooster, 1996) as a consequence of the legislation, increased provision and growing expertise and skills on the part of early years workers and practitioners (Wolfendale, 1997a; Wolfendale, 2000).

A number of key areas will now be examined which will, it is hoped, provide exemplars and evidence of continued and positive movement towards theoretically robust and coherent Early Years/SEN policies and practice.

Assessment and Curriculum

The range of approaches to EY assessment, such as direct observation of children at play or involved in specific learning tasks, systematic record-keeping, checklist completion, cognitive testing can be carried out by mainstream EY practitioners and those involved in identifying special needs. What I suggest could be regarded as distinctive features in assessing for individual special needs, whether it is intrinsically part of overall assessment for all, such as Baseline Assessment on entry to school or a parallel, or indeed separate activity in time and/or place are:

- *close* focus on specific behaviours;

- relation of these to overall functioning and ecological factors and influences;

- contextualising a child's functioning with reference to available/needed classroom/institutional human and material resources;

- the requirement to share and act upon assessment information with all key players in a child's life.

Assessment principles as espoused by Nutbrown (1996) and in Wolfendale (1997, p.6) provide an overarching and inclusive framework for assessment of all young children. Hinton (1993) is emphatic that fundamental principles and practices of EY assessment (cf. Drummond & Nutbrown, 1996) must apply to all children. Within this universal framework there should be the provision and opportunity for further differential, focused assessment for SEN, as outlined above. The message from seasoned EY practitioners is that 'acts of assessment' are continuous within an early years setting and clear, sophisticated recording techniques are a prerequisite.

Hinton averred that 'the best assessment practices being developed in preschool provision are improving our ability to identify special needs' (1993, p.52). The inclusion of special needs into Baseline Assessment approaches (one of the key accreditation criteria, SCAA/QCA, 1997) reflects this view.

But - as we would all agree - the raison d'être of assessment is that it should inform and support curriculum planning. However, up to now an inclusive approach has been hard to achieve. There have been many texts on early years education and on curriculum approaches which barely mention special needs (cf. Curtis, 1998; Wood & Attfield, 1996). Furthermore, schisms and disagreements about the form, content and emphases of early learning opportunities have raged between practitioners, researchers and policy-makers for years, in textbooks (and see Hurst and Joseph, 1998, for espousal of a developmentally appropriate curriculum), at conferences and in the media. Early years curriculum blueprints abound therefore, one of the most recent being 'Quality in diversity in early learning' a carefully researched document, and a collaborative work by members of the Early Childhood Education Forum (ECEF/NCB, 1998).

But the one most likely to dominate is the just-published 'official' QCA document entitled 'Early Learning Goals' (QCA, 1999), which supersedes the Desirable Learning Outcomes. This blueprint, which will come into force in September 2000, is intended for 3-5 year-olds, includes children in the Reception year, and this age-phase is to be called the *Foundation Stage*. The document sets out principles and entitlements, common features of good practice, the six areas of learning and addresses 'the diverse needs of children'.

It is notable that the page and a half devoted to 'special educational needs and disabilities' (pp. 12, 13) are more detailed than the ELG precursor, the Desirable Learning Outcomes. Furthermore, exemplar material in the ELG documents (as well as the detailed guidance planned for publication in the summer of 2000) includes young children with a range of SEN.

Cross-reference between ELG and the revised SEN Code of Practice betokens alignment of the hitherto disparate areas of EY and SEN assessment and curriculum approaches (also see DfEE, 1998b, for a 'bridging' approach).

Early Intervention and Prevention - towards an inclusive framework
Early intervention typically has these primary goals:

- to support families to support their children's development;

- to promote children's development in key domains (cognitive, social, physical, emotional, linguistic) via early years curriculum and learning opportunities;

- to promote children's coping competence;

- to prevent the emergence of future problems.

In the Early Years/SEN realm intervention is purposeful and designed to effect as close a match as possible between a young child's identified special needs and that provision or resource which will meet his or her needs and best facilitate learning and development. The interventions should manifestly *make a difference* (see Soriano, 1998, for a review of early intervention trends in 17 European countries).

In a keynote speech at a conference on early intervention (Bayley, 1999), the Minister, Paul Boateng, stated that the Government's political agenda in this field includes early intervention, healthy living, community support, multi-agency working and a focus on families. Specifically, the ideals are translated into initiatives (some already mentioned above) such as Education and Health Action Zones, Early Excellence Centres, Childcare Partnerships, SURE START, parenting support, action on school exclusion and many others. Finally, after many years, there is acknowledgement that co-ordinated 'top down' policies are the vital prerequisite for 'on the ground' action, and there is, then, a contemporary view that children's services should be *targeted* to those children who, within a generalised concept of 'need',

a) have early-appearing/early-identified disabilities and special (educational) needs;

b) are deemed to be vulnerable and at risk by virtue of a); and/or who

c) live in milieux of social and economic deprivation and disadvantage.

The definition of inclusion as expressed by Widdows (1997) encapsulates the broadest areas of service delivery to young children and their families:

> '... it embraces the functioning of families and of societies. In the context of families with disabled children, especially young children, it

covers such everyday but important issues as the role of families and friends, and the assistance and support they provide; the impact of disability and non-disabled siblings; the practicality of getting out and about on family outings; the way in which intervention is organised; and the impact of attitudes held by the general public' (p.12).

This is the context within which Dickens and Denziloe (1998) couch their myriad practical proposals as to how to operate inclusion within early years settings. Their handbook outlines inclusion principles before detailing their proposals within a range of assessment and curriculum areas.

In Widdows' definition of inclusion, partnership with parents/families with young children is intrinsic and a bedrock part of the formulation.

The transition of the erstwhile view that parents are clients and recipients of services towards a view that they should be partners in the planning and delivery of services has been well chronicled (Wolfendale, 1992; 1997b). The philosophy of partnership is expressed within the 1994 SEN *Code of Practice* and the previous Government encouraged parent-professional partnership through various means including the Parent Partnership Scheme, which was evaluated for the DfEE by Wolfendale and Cook (1997) and which has been further encouraged by the present Government by its inclusion within the SEN Programme of Action.

Such realisation that parents are informed experts on their children is belated but totally welcome, as is the recognition that parental representation must form part of local early years partnerships.

However, whether or not truly egalitarian models of parental partnership pertain, for young children with SEN, the 'primary professional role is to support the family in making decisions and stating individual preferences regarding services for their children' (Talay-Ongan, 1998, p.297).

It must be acknowledged in passing, regrettably there is not the space in this paper to explore the direct participation of young children as a fundamental part of an inclusion model. There is a burgeoning literature on this area (and see Wolfendale, 2000) Chapter 1 for a review of approaches to involving young children in expressing their views about their own development and learning).

Personnel and Staffing - the distinctive contribution of early years practitioners

To people unversed in early years provision, there must seem to be a bewildering array of early years and SEN workers in a confusing plethora of settings (see Roffey, 1999). Early Years Development and Childcare Partnerships will, of course, over time, rationalise and streamline the provision. However, it remains the case that many specialists and experts are to be found within and between providers and agencies, each with distinctive roles and responsibilities. This has been a debating issue for years - to what extent do roles and duties overlap and duplicate; are differing training routes incompatible with each other; can 'best value' service be offered with a proliferation of professionals?

An additional reality factor is this: there is a rapidly accumulating stock of knowledge and research findings about early years development, and the splitting into specialisms of specific special needs, e.g. autism, dyslexia, physical disability - these and others require considerable time and effort on anyone's part to stay abreast of theory, research, applications. Likewise, there is an onus on the part of all early years workers to take account of other innovations and policies that impact upon early provision, such as the National Literacy and Numeracy Strategies, Baseline Assessment, Early Learning Goals, and SEN assessment and curriculum approaches.

As part of EY/SEN Policy formulation (see below), there has to be an overarching coalition of the key 'primary players' in any local EY/SEN realms and a co-ordinated approach to training and professional development, which cannot in the future, I suggest, only be left to individual choice of areas to professionally develop but must be based on collective needs assessment.

Assuring Quality and Effectiveness in Early Years Provision

Ways of measuring quality in early years and SEN were explored in Wolfendale (1997a) and this review confirmed that there are a number of models and mechanisms in both these areas.

There is now increasing emphasis upon *evidence-based practice*, in assessing intentions and outcomes as well as the quality of services (Macdonald & Roberts, 1995; NCB Highlight No. 170, 1999). Such an approach behoves all early years providers initially to adhere closely to the guidance on Early Years Development and Childcare Partnerships (DfEE, 1998c) especially in respect of SEN (Annexe 8, p.30), to set clear goals for curriculum planning and intervention approaches, devise outcome measures and means of evaluating these strategies.

There is ever-increasing emphasis upon accountability of professional activities and the broad context here is the set of responsibilities for SEN that local education authorities (LEAs) have and must be seen to exercise equitably (Audit Commission, 1999).

An Encompassing View of Childhood and of Meeting Young Children's Needs

Nowadays, theoretical formulations of childhood do not exclude, as a separate category, children with special needs - inclusivity means taking an overarching view of similar, perhaps universal learning, social, other needs of all children, at whatever fast or slower developmental pace they progress. Differentiation means responding sensitively at critical points in time towards individual children. Wilson (1998), an exponent of this view, refers to 'teachable moments', a familiar notion to early years workers, which surely apply to all children. She also draws attention to a historical separation between the traditions of early childhood educators and those of special educators and proposes a realignment and merger of these two disciplines.

The key element of her proposed merger is to move beyond 'multidisciplinary' approaches in which practitioners/professionals work alongside each other (but retain their own approaches) towards a 'trans-disciplinary' model. This would require a significant shift for practitioners in the United Kingdom and Ruth Wilson's model is defined and outlined below, to promote and stimulate debate about its efficacy in practice. She writes:

> 'Trans-discipline involves a crossing of disciplinary lines, a stretching of one's professional role, and the development of additional competencies. For the early childhood educator, this means learning more about children with special needs and developing the skills to effectively modify the programme for them. For the early childhood special educator this means learning more about human development during the early childhood years, becoming more familiar with the intricacies of developmentally appropriate practices, and learning how to work with a larger group of children with varying interests and abilities.' (p.15)

But perhaps this model is not so radical, proposed as it is at a time when support services are moving closer to each other, in ethos, principles and goals. As stated in McNair (1998) 'many people now expect to work in more than one occupational arena with children and young people during their working lives. The development of the responsive, reflective and skilful practitioner is a challenge faced by everyone' (p.68). The Interdisciplinary Framework conceptualised within this (McNair) publication is based on the assumption that all those who work with children and young people need similar underpinning knowledge and understanding. The working metaphor for the Framework is the concept of cog wheels - move one and all others move. The 'cogwheel' represents the developmental nature of childhood within its social and cultural context (see Wolfendale 2000, Ch. 1 for discussion).

Policy Options for Special Needs in the Early Years

'The full benefits of investment in children are genuinely immeasurable. Any arguments produced to support investment in our children in essence remain value-based' (Lloyd, Hemingway, Newman, Roberts & Webster, 1997, p.11).

This quotation encapsulates the humanitarian, ethical, societal, pedagogic rationales for early years services, which must surely underpin local and national policies. At the beginning of this paper, I expressed the intention to try to effect a realignment of hitherto disparate worlds of early years and special needs. We can applaud and celebrate those contemporary innovations which epitomise an inclusive approach, and hopefully can identify rather more problematic areas that need resolution.

In this paper a number of specific areas of policy and practice have been examined. See the figure on the next page for a visual statement of the interrelationships between policy, provision and practice. Consistent with a focus on SEN and early years as an area in its own right, NASEN has developed and endorsed a Policy on Early Years which contains the ingredients for collective responsibilities at local and national levels. It begins with Key Principles, and outlines differential responsibilities of schools, Local Authorities, Health, Social Services and Government. It could provide a blueprint for adoption.

In general, policies should reflect young children's unique circumstances and needs and how adults and society attempt to provide for these. We bequeath these ideas and strategies to future early years workers in the new century.

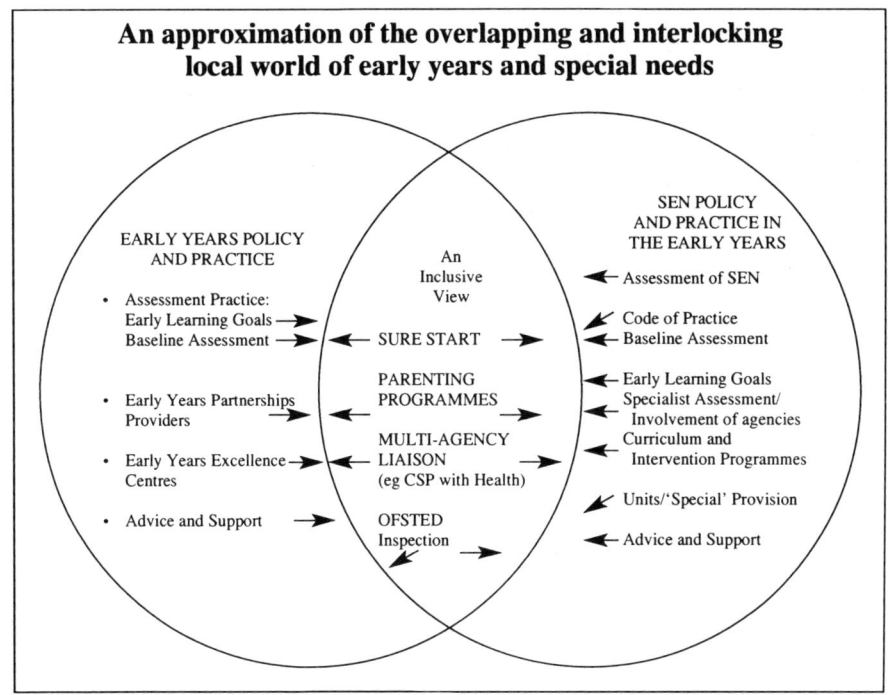

References

Audit Commission (1999) *Held in Trust, the LEA of the Future*, 1 Vincent Square, London SW1P 2PN.

Bayley, R. (Ed.) (1999) *Transforming Children's Lives: the importance of early intervention*, Family Policy Studies Centre, 9 Tavistock Place, London WC1H 9SN.

Curtis, A. (1998) *A Curriculum for the pre-school child*, 2nd edition, London: Routledge.

Department for Education and Employment (1998a) *Meeting SEN: A Programme of Action*, London: Stationery Office.

Department for Education and Employment (1998b) *Supporting the Target-Setting Process*, London: DfEE.

Department for Education and Employment (1998c) *Early Years Development and Childcare Partnership, planning guidance 1999-2000*, London: Stationery Office.

Dickens, M. and Denziloe, J. (1998) *All together - how to create inclusive services for disabled children and their families, a practical handbook for early years workers*, National Early Years Network, 77 Holloway Road, London N7 8JZ.

Drummond, M. J. and Nutbrown, C. (1996) *Observing and assessing young children*, in Pugh, G. (Ed.) Contemporary Issues in the Early Years, 2nd edition, London: Paul Chapman.

Early Childhood Education Forum (1998) *Quality in Diversity in Early Learning, a framework for early childhood practitioners*, London: National Children's Bureau.

Glass, N. (1999) 'SURE START: The Development of an Early Intervention Programme for Young Children in the UK', *Children and Society*, Vol. 13, No. 4, September, 257-265.

Hinton, S. (1993) 'Assessing for Special Needs and Supporting Learning in the early years and nursery education', Chapter 3 in Wolfendale, S. (Ed.) *Assessing Special Educational Needs*, London: Cassell.

Hurst, V. and Joseph, J. (1998) *Supporting Early Learning, the Way Forward*, Buckingham: Open University Press.

Lloyd, E., Hemingway, M., Newman, T., Roberts, H. and Webster, A. (1997) *Today and Tomorrow, investing in our Children*, Barnardos, Tanners Lane, Barkingside, Ilford, Essex IG6 1QG.

Macdonald, G. and Roberts, H. (1995) *What works in the early years: effective interventions for children and their families in health, social welfare, education and child protection.* Barnardos, Tanners Lane, Barkingside, Ilford, Essex IG6 1QG.

McNair, S. (Ed.) (1998) *Developing Disciplines. The experience of the Discipline Networks Programme 1995-1998*, Suffolk, DfEE Stationery Office.

NASEN (1998) *Baseline Assessment: Benefits and Pitfalls*, Policy Paper 3 of SEN Policy Options Steering Group, Tamworth: NASEN.

NASEN (1999) *Policy on Early Years*, Tamworth: NASEN.

NCB Highlight No. 170 (1999) *Evidence-based Child Care Practice*, London: National Children's Bureau.

Nutbrown, C. (Ed.) (1996) *Children's Rights and Early Education*, London: Paul Chapman.

Qualifications and Curriculum Authority (QCA) *The National Framework for Baseline Assessment; criteria and procedures for the Accreditation of Baseline Assessment Schemes*, Bolton Street, London W1Y 7PD.

Qualifications and Curriculum Authority (QCA) (1999) *Early Learning Goals*, Bolton Street, London W1Y 7PD (supersedes *Desirable Learning Outcomes*).

Roffey, S. (1999) *Special Needs in the Early Years, Collaboration, Communication and Co-ordination*, London: David Fulton Publishers.

Rumbold, A. (Chair) *Starting with Quality*, Report of the Commission of Enquiry into the Quality of Educational Experience offered to 3-5 year olds, London: HMSO.

Soriano, V. (Ed.) (1998) *Early Intervention in Europe, trends in 17 European Countries*, European Agency for Development in Special Needs Education, Middelfart: Denmark.

Talay-Ongan, A. (1998) *Typical and atypical development in early childhood*, Leicester: British Psychological Society Books.

Wade, B. and Moore, M. (2000) 'Starting Early with Books', in Wolfendale, S. and Bastiani, J. (Eds.) *The Contribution of Parents to School Effectiveness*, London: David Fulton Publishers.

Widdows, J. (1997) *A Special Need for Inclusion*, London: Children's Society.

Wilson, R. (1998) *Special Educational Needs in the Early Years*, London: Routledge.

Wolfendale, S. (1992) *Empowering Parents and Teaching - Working for Children*, London: Cassell.

Wolfendale, S. (Ed.) (1993) *Assessing Special Educational Needs*, London: Cassell.

Wolfendale, S. (Ed.) (1997a) *Meeting Special Needs in the Early Years, directions in Policy and Practice*, London: David Fulton Publishers.

Wolfendale, S. (Ed.) (1997b) *Working with Parents of SEN children after the Code of Practice*, London: David Fulton Publishers.

Wolfendale, S. (Ed.) (2000) *Special Needs in the Early Years, snapshots of practice*, London: Routledge.

Wolfendale, S. and Cook, G. (1997) *Evaluation of SEN Parent Partnership Schemes*, DfEE Research Report No. 34, DfEE Publications, PO Box 5050, Sudbury, Suffolk CO10 6ZQ.

Wolfendale, S. and Einzig, H. (Eds.) (1999) *Parenting Education and Support, new opportunities*, London: David Fulton Publishers.

Wolfendale, S. and Wooster, J. (1996) 'Meeting Special Needs in the Early Years', in Pugh, G. (Ed.) *Contemporary Issues in the Early Years*, London: Paul Chapman.

Wood, E. and Attfield, J. (1996) *Play, Learning and the Early Childhood Curriculum*, London: Paul Chapman.

Chapter 3
Developing a Comprehensive and Integrated Approach to Early Years Services for Children with Special Educational Needs – Opportunities and Challenges in Current Government Initiatives

PHILIPPA RUSSELL, Council for Disabled Children

'When we introduced Early Years Development Partnerships last year, we said it was just the beginning, that early years education ought not to be looked at in isolation, that the needs of families and the community were changing; and that our aim was to develop a comprehensive and integrated approach to good quality early years education and childcare.'

Margaret Hodge, introducing *Early Years Development and Childcare Partnership Planning Guidance 1999-2000*.

Policies for Excellence: Implications of the Programme of Action for Children with Special Educational Needs in the Early Years

The United Kingdom, like the United States, has seen an ongoing debate over several decades about what constitutes effective early identification and intervention strategies for young children with special educational needs or disabilities. Evaluation of strategies like the USA's Highscope Programme have indicated that the benefits of early intervention can be long-term and have significant impact upon the adult lives of the children (and families) concerned. The Programme of Action on SEN acknowledges the importance of the early years and promises to:

> 'provide high quality early years education and childcare, including support for parents, and encourage earlier identification of difficulties and appropriate early intervention'.

These goals are to be progressively achieved through Early Years Development Partnerships, which integrate childcare and education (described below); a greater emphasis upon earlier identification with appropriate interventions to tackle difficulties and effective support (including independent advice) for parents from the earliest stages. Baseline assessment should offer a planned transition from pre-school to the school stages of education. There is a new and welcome emphasis upon multi-agency planning and provision for children with special educational needs (with Early Years Excellence Centres offering models for such collaborative working and for the inclusion of children with a range of disabilities and special needs within mainstream provision).

Early years provision in the United Kingdom has always reflected diversity, with Education, Health, Social Services Departments, the independent and voluntary sectors all making a range of provision. Local authorities have varying levels of direct maintained education provision in the early years, with some authorities relying heavily upon the voluntary and independent sectors. Over the past decade there has been growing concern about how best to integrate education and childcare and to support *all* early years providers (whether offering home-based individual care as through childminders at one end of the spectrum or offering a range of group care or educational provision through the Pre-School Learning Alliance in the voluntary sector or maintained nursery classes or schools).

The integration of care with education within the Early Years Partnerships and within a growing range of providers offers both challenges and opportunities. The publication of the desirable Early Learning Goals has led to a powerful debate about:

- definitions of *excellence and inclusion* in early years services;

- the *purpose* of early years education;

- the need to ensure that children have access to *play* and other developmental activities;

- concerns about *SEN expertise in early years provision and sources of advice and support* which will be available to the increasingly diverse early years sector.

The education of young children with special educational needs cannot be achieved without active participation of parents and a wider range of community services. Definitions are still challenging. The current debate about what constitutes *inclusion*; the role of *specialist* provision and support services and the interface between *play* and early years education is still unresolved.

But there are real opportunities for the development of a more proactive approach to planning and delivering services for young children with SEN/disabilities across early years services. The key Government initiatives are described below and within the Early Years Development and Childcare Partnerships, Sure Start and Quality Protects there are encouraging and innovative approaches to identification and intervention for children with a range of special needs. Other major opportunities roll on behind. The *NHS Act 1999* introduces 'partnership in action', offering new flexibilities in joint commissioning and pooled budgets which could help bridge the gap between education and child health services in many authorities. New integrated inspection arrangements within the Care Standards Bill extend the Government's key theme of quality and regular audit and review.

Importantly, the theme of partnership with parents runs across all the strands of the Government's early years projects. With specific reference to special educational needs, proposals to extend the role of Parent Partnership Services to the early years sector is a reminder of the potential isolation of parents with young children with special educational needs and the importance of strengthening parents' confidence and competence in helping their young children to learn and develop.

Finally and by no means least, the advent of Human Rights legislation and the creation of a Disability Rights Commission in 2000 have reminded many providers of new responsibilities under Part III of the *Disability Discrimination Act* - and the need to ensure that early years services are truly accessible and as far as possible inclusive for children with disabilities, and disabled parents, carers and staff.

The Government announced its broad policy approach to early years services in May 1997. The key element within the new policy direction was the requirement that every local authority should create a broad-based Early Years Partnership, which would draw up an Early Years Development Plan for the area. The Education Development Plan became the Early Years Development and Childcare Plan in 1998, when the Government published *Meeting the Childcare Challenge* (DfEE, 1998b), a Green Paper setting out a National Childcare Strategy for children aged 0-14 years. The Green Paper recognised the *'vital links between education and childcare in the early years'* and proposed that the National Strategy should be planned and delivered by local partnerships. These partnerships built upon the earlier *Early years Development Partnerships* which now became *Early Years Development and Childcare Partnerships*. Their statutory basis is contained within Sections 117-124 of the *Schools Standards and Framework Act 1998*.

The emphasis upon local partnerships and strategic direction was put firmly within the context of targets and *'strategic principles'* for Early Years Development and Childcare Partnerships. The 1999-2000 guidance sets as targets:

- A good quality free early education place for all 4 year-olds whose parents want one (LEAs having a duty to secure such places from April 1999) and an agreed percentage of 3 year-olds by 2001-2.

- Good affordable childcare for children aged 0-14 in every neighbourhood.

Services in education and child care must meet the Government's guiding principles of:

- **Quality** (with clear criteria regarding minimum standards and more uniform regulation across sectors with associated inspection, self-assessment and action planning arrangements);

- **A clear framework of qualifications** for both early years education and childcare workers;

- **Active involvement of parents and family in early education and childcare**, with the opportunity to improve skills;

- **A qualified teacher** to be involved in all settings providing early years education within an Early Years Development and Childcare Plan (EYDCP).

The guidance expects that early years services offering education or childcare should represent:

- **Diversity** (with provision being made across private, public and the voluntary sectors);

- **Inclusive education or childcare** for children with disabilities or SEN *'where possible and appropriate'*;

- **Equal opportunities** for children and families from different cultural, ethnic and religious backgrounds;

- **Accessibility** to where children and families live or work, integrating education with childcare where possible;

- **Information** for parents, carers, employers and providers on full range of options and sources of advice and support;

- **'Evidence-based planning'** - all partnerships are required to carry out audits of the range of local provision, to identify strengths and weaknesses and to plan accordingly;

- **Partnership** in planning local provision (with private and voluntary sectors active members of partnerships).

Planning for Special Educational Needs within the EYDCP

Annex Eight of the EYDCP sets out specific information on special educational needs. The partnerships must set out:

- details of the support which will be provided to ensure that all early years education providers are able to identify and address special educational needs;

- information about the childcare and early education provision available locally for children with special educational needs or with disabilities (including any special support, such as the LEA's support services);

- the partnership's plans for making provision more inclusive;

- details of any specialist training available locally for early years education and childcare staff working with children with special educational needs or with disabilities (including training shared between the sectors);

- details of information and advice available to parents and other carers about child care and early education for children with disabilities or special educational needs.

An important new requirement within the guidance for the second year of EYDCPs is the reminder that childcare provision made through the independent or voluntary or Social Services/Health sectors is covered by Part III of the *Disability Discrimination Act 1995* (DDA) (Part III being implemented in October 1999). Maintained education services are currently outside the provisions of DDA, but the Disability Task Force (1999) has recommended that the Government should address this anomaly as a matter of priority. The Government, launching the Task Force's Report, has undertaken to take action in the forthcoming SEN Bill.

Maintained schools and nurseries are covered with reference to employment practice, the provision of information and access to school premises for 'non-educational' meetings (e.g. parent evenings, leasing of school premises or social activities and clubs after school). Hence training and support for early years services must address the new dimension of potential disability discrimination and the wider human rights issues relating to the implementation of the *Human Rights Act* in 2000.

Sure Start

Sure Start has been rightly described by David Blunkett as *'one of the most ambitious early intervention programmes ever created in the United Kingdom ... a cornerstone of the Government's drive to tackle child poverty and social exclusion, based on firm evidence of "what works"*. The Government has invested £452 million to set up 250 Sure Start projects across England within the life of the current Parliament. The programme aims to improve the health and well-being (and thereby the life chances) of families and children before and after birth through providing new and often pioneering services offering:

- family support;

- advice on nurturing;

- better access to health care;

- new opportunities for early learning.

The first trailblazer Sure Start programmes have been established in 60 areas and a further 69 districts are submitting proposals. Precisely because the programme addresses:

> 'The promotion of the physical, intellectual and social development of pre-school children - particularly those who are disadvantaged - to ensure that they are ready to thrive when they get to school',

it has enormous potential for 'modelling' new and innovative approaches to working with young children and families experiencing difficulties in parenting or in development and learning. Key targets for Sure Start areas include:

- ensuring that 90% of children have normal speech and language development at 18 months and three years;

- ensuring that 100% of children have access to good quality play and early learning opportunities, helping progress towards early learning goals when they get to school.

The experiences of the first trailblazer projects have informed the guidance for the second round. An analysis of the first project plans indicated the need for greater clarity in guidance about disability and special educational needs and programmes are now expected to set out:

- the different provision and services which are available for children with disabilities or special educational needs and their families;

- details of arrangements made by service providers for the early identification and assessment of children's special educational needs;

- details of any specialist provision and services (and the assessment and referral arrangements to such services).

There is a strong emphasis upon preventive services, with a *Sure Start Guide to Evidence-Based Practice* to offer examples of how early identification and assessment services or support for children with complex needs might work in practice.

As with the Early Years Development and Childcare Partnerships, Sure Start projects are reminded of their responsibilities under the *Disability Discrimination Act*. Projects are also reminded of the importance of providing a range of information, advice, befriending and advocacy services for families - a reminder that the Government proposes to strengthen the role of Parent Partnership Services to work with early years services and parents of younger children rather than focusing solely upon the school stages of education.

Quality Protects

'Social services have a crucial role to play within the Government's wider social inclusion strategy ... Children's social services work with some of the most disadvantaged families and some of the most vulnerable children in our society. Children's social services need to provide the right targeted help to ensure that all children and young people are able to take maximum advantage of universal services, in particular education and health. Good assessment of the needs of children and families plays an important role here, enabling needs to be identified at an early stage so that services and support can be provided.' (*The Government's Objectives for Children's Social Services*, 1999b, DoH)

The three-year Quality Protects initiative was launched in September 1998. The programme arose from widespread concerns about the safety and quality of care offered to vulnerable children (in particular those looked after by the local authority) raised in the Utting Children's Safeguard Review. The programme has four key elements, as listed below.

- **New national objectives** setting standards and outcomes for services for children in need. One such objective will necessitate close partnerships with education and child health services and has implications for policies across early years services, namely that,

    'Children with specific social needs arising out of disability or a health condition should be living in families or other appropriate settings in the community where their assessed needs [for education, health or social care] are adequately met and reviewed.'

- **Annual Management Action Plans** (QMAPs) which set out how each local authority will strengthen and improve their services so that they meet the new objectives.

- **A new Children's Grant of £375 million** to fund improvements.

- **A new and important role for elected members** in setting standards and ensuring that local authorities meet them.

The first round of Quality Protects 'QMAPs' were jointly developed and signed up to by Education and Social Services Departments. The second round will also require participation by the relevant local health services. All planning arrangements under Quality Protects must address services and support for disabled children. An analysis of the first round of QMAPs (Khan & Russell, 1999) indicates some creative new thinking about children with disabilities and special educational needs within a more holistic local authority planning system. However, the same analysis indicates the challenges in planning across education and social care and in ensuring that the necessary supports are available for the greater inclusion of children with a range of special needs within mainstream services. Some key messages from this first analysis are set out below under the commentary on current Government initiatives.

Opportunities and Challenges: The Implications of New Initiatives for Children with Disabilities or Special Educational Needs in the Early Years

The opportunities within Quality Protects, Sure Start and the Early Years Development and Childcare Partnerships to improve the access of young children with disability or special educational needs are considerable. The principles for early years education set out in *Early Learning Goals* (QCA/DfEE, 1999) state that:

> 'No child should be excluded or disadvantaged because of his or her race, culture or religion, home language, family background, special educational needs, gender or disability.'

But the sheer diversity of early years provision and rising expectations about quality and quantity of such provision (with many parents wanting what Ministers have called 'wrap-around' education and care) raises some important issues.

The Council for Disabled Children's analysis of the first year's Management Action Plans for Quality Protects, together with information received from members with reference to Early Years Development and Child Care Partnerships and Sure Start, highlights some of those issues, but also some innovative partnerships and initiatives.

Some key challenges and issues include:

- **Definitions of disability and special educational needs** (in particular determining criteria for the allocation of resources at stage three of assessment and without going through statutory assessment procedures). New guidance for Early Years Partnerships and Sure Start reminds providers of their responsibilities under the *Disability Discrimination Act 1995*. The implementation of Part III of the DDA (Access to goods and services) raises important issues for early years providers in terms of defining access; considering what *reasonable adjustments* might be required to offer a more inclusive service and addressing major issues with regard to disability equality training and policies and procedures which present positive images of disability.

- **Developing inclusive services**. Early years services should offer unique opportunities to develop and 'model' inclusive services. The majority of children with SEN or disabilities will already be in early years provision when their special need is first identified. Inclusion in the early years will also ensure that children and parents are part of local community services and will hopefully develop natural networks of support. However, as the Green Paper (1998) noted, inclusion is a process not a single state. Placements which are unsupported and poorly planned may deskill children with disabilities or special needs. The outreach role of specialist and support services will be critical to create confidence across a diverse range of providers and to provide any necessary early intervention. Early analysis of some EYDCPs and Quality Protects MAPs indicates that inclusion is a general policy commitment. But clarity about how it should be supported is still variable across public, private and voluntary sectors.

- **Reflecting cultural diversity**. Any discussion of inclusion must address the cultural diversity of many communities and the importance of reflecting such cultural diversity within the development of local services for children with special educational needs. Quality Protects MAPs and EYDCPs indicate some interesting partnerships with local minority ethnic groups in improving the accessibility and appropriateness of services - but they also indicate major gaps in provision, a new study from the Joseph Rowntree Foundation clearly demonstrating the greater vulnerability of families from minority ethnic groups in terms of access to services for children with disabilities or special educational needs.

- **Strategic planning**. Few local authorities have reliable databases on the numbers of children with disabilities or special educational needs in their area. Early Years Development and Childcare Partnerships vary in the extent to which they have strong disability/special educational needs representation and the integration of child care and education has been challenging.

- **SEN policies**. A critical issue in effective strategic planning will be the availability of reliable information on policy and practice within services and also within individual provider units. The maintained education sector will have SEN policies and such policies offer valuable information for monitoring, review and ultimately inspection. They also inform parents and local authorities about the *capacity* and *aspirations* of an individual provider in addressing special educational needs and disability. SEN policies are variable in the independent and voluntary sectors, one independent provider (personal communication) commenting that:

> 'In my LEA, pressures on support services mean that there is little advice or assistance for nurseries like my own which wish to address SEN more proactively. We would welcome clearer guidance about what sort of policy we should develop and how to translate it into practice. EYDCPs could do more to support SEN providers in their area - some do, but in our new unitary authority, this has not been a priority.'

- **Quality assurance: standards and inspection.** Some Early Years Partnerships have clear quality assurance procedures, setting specific targets which include accurate data collection to ensure that services are planned on the basis of ascertainable need. But others have experienced greater difficulty in setting up such procedures. Targets set in other initiatives are not necessarily matched to those in Early Years Partnerships. The Care Standards Bill raises a number of important issues regarding joint inspections, not least the assurance that the new assessment arrangements will take account of special educational needs and disability across all sectors and that there will be sufficient SEN expertise within the new inspection teams.

There has been growing interest in standard setting (with some voluntary organisations taking a lead in defining quality services for particular disabilities or special educational needs). The National Deaf Children's Society (1999), in setting quality standards in education, comments that it is essential to have:

> 'Standards designed to be a flexible tool for use by professionals and services aiming to provide a high-quality service ... which can be used in a national context to monitor the development of services nationally and provide feedback on expected levels of service.'

The National Deaf Children's Society acknowledges the potential role of the Early Years Partnerships in setting standards and monitoring progress for *all* young children in their area and also highlights the importance of understanding the context within which standards will be set, endorsing the use of audits to 'map' local provision and identify strengths and weaknesses.

- **The relationship between the LEA and other providers.** Both Quality Protects and Early Years Development and Childcare Partnerships have acknowledged the challenge of providing advice and support on special educational needs across a diversity of providers. Some authorities have tackled the challenge positively. Cornwall extends LEA support services to the non-maintained sector, with requests being processed through the Business Manager of their Early Years Service. Barnsley, Islington and Kent have pools of peripatetic skilled staff, equipment and resources which can be rapidly deployed on an outreach basis. Havering's Early Years Development and Childcare Partnership is creating support networks of SENCos across the private and voluntary sectors to encourage shared learning and peer support. But there is continuing work to be done in many authorities with regard to information on local support services for the full range of providers and how it may be accessed.

- **Early intervention.** In the USA, as in the United Kingdom, there has been ongoing interest in early intervention. The evidence base for 'what works' in early intervention (including family support as well as child focussed early education programmes) is limited. The Mental Health Foundation, in commissioning a review of early intervention strategies for young children with learning disabilities and challenging behaviours (1997), noted the lack of research evidence on the effectiveness of different approaches to early intervention and the need for more longitudinal evaluations in the United Kingdom to mirror those carried out in the USA.

In the USA, evaluations of Highscope and Headstart clearly demonstrate the dual benefits of support for parents through education, day care and practical help and specific programmes to encourage children's development and learning. Sure Start's key objectives reflect the USA interest in holistic approaches to families across designated local communities, with a strong emphasis upon engaging *parents* as co-educators and as development workers in disadvantaged local communities.

A Headstart programme in Georgetown, Washington (personal communication) estimates that 69% of its parent supporters and educators are themselves 'graduates' of early intervention programmes. Hence the programme is rolled out across generations in deprived communities. One parent participant (personal communication) commented that:

'Having a child with special needs was not what I expected. We had enough problems as a family, no work, bad housing, my husband coming off drugs. I'd left school at 15, I didn't feel I could face special needs. But Headstart valued me. The programme really helped the whole family. We couldn't start on education until the rest of our lives were sorted out.'

- **Assessment issues**. Sure Start and EYDCPs are expected to set out clearly their arrangements for the identification and assessment of children with special educational needs or disabilities and to clarify their relationships with the relevant LEA. In practice, identification and assessment present particular challenges in the early years. The National Deaf Children's Society (1999), looking at assessment in early years provision, notes that:

    'Good early years assessment will develop from effective and child-centred assessment. Parents should have the right to expect high-quality and comprehensive assessment of their child's needs in the early years by professionals fully aware of the educational, social and developmental implications of the disability or special educational need.'

In practice, early years assessment in the context of new initiatives is challenging. Assessment will need to address a broad range of objectives, including play and development; support for families; the development of language, speech and competence in communication (a high priority for the Sure Start Programme) as well as educational placement in the early years. One voluntary sector provider (personal communication) observed that:

'Early years assessment challenges everyone. "False positives" are devastating to families. Sometimes we need to assess the family rather than the child. Many of us are unsure what information we should provide for baseline assessment.'

'I have had enormous support from my LEA's own support services. They have ensured that we all understand how local assessment and support arrangements work. Additional resources are available for the voluntary and independent sectors. Without such investment by the LEA, I believe we would have seen a major new demand for Statements for young children with SEN. As it is, we can work together. I have valued the new initiatives because sometimes family poverty, isolation, poor housing are the real barriers to progress.'

- **A new training agenda**. QCAs work in establishing a national framework of accredited qualifications for early years services will play a critical role in achieving quality across early years services for children with special educational needs. The integration of education, childcare and play within a common early years framework has created national debate (with particular concern about the need to safeguard the play element within educational programmes for young children).

Integrating training across early years education and childcare can be challenging. Many Early Years Partnerships have developed training strategies, one noting (personal communication) that:

> 'The United Kingdom will need to move towards the European 'social pedagogy' approach to early years training, recognising that early years staff in education and social services must reinforce and contribute to each other's expertise. If we believe that effective early years education is interdependent with social care, play and family circumstances, then we have to ensure that we develop a new training agenda.'

Training for diversity has created difficulties, though some authorities have taken a strategic approach. Richmond offers specialist training in SEN to childminders and a range of support staff (including befrienders or volunteers as appropriate). Other authorities like Southampton have utilised peer support, with the local Childminders' Network having one trained team member who can advise and support on special educational needs.

An important trend in 'modelling' good practice and in offering outreach training and support has been the development of the Early Years Excellence Centres, many of which both prioritise disability and special educational needs and which have the capacity to support development in local services. A playgroup co-ordinator (personal communication) noted that for her:

> 'The Early Years Excellence Centre gave me both the training and the direct contact with services for children with SEN which we - a

voluntary organisation in a rural area - urgently needed. Our staff were able to share training activities and we all felt our professional development grew. Now we have an SEN policy and we have increased the numbers of children with disabilities and special educational needs. We also get better support from the LEA because we now know what we need and we can use their support services better.'

- **Supporting parents - the role of the voluntary sector.** The Government's Programme of Action on SEN, like EYDCPs, Sure Start and Quality Protects, highlights the central role of parents in early years education and child care. The forthcoming SEN Bill is expected to not only strengthen the role of Parent Partnership Services, but to extend their role to the early years sector. Many voluntary organisations are not only providers, but also offer training, support and policy input at local and national levels.

Empowering parents of children with disabilities or SEN in the early years can be challenging. Portage has demonstrated the effectiveness of parents' roles as co-educators and home teachers. Voluntary organisations may provide a wide range of support services, information and advice. But not all parents are natural joiners. Government policy expects consultation with service users (children as well as parents) and some EYDCPs have developed a range of consultation mechanisms to ensure that their services are offered flexibly, appropriately and reflect parents' needs.

The balance between education and child care will continue to be a subject for debate. Parents at Work (1999), reporting on a national survey of parents of disabled children wishing to enter paid employment, indicates the current dearth of integrated provision for parents of children with disabilities or SEN. The trend towards paid employment for mothers with young children has implications for the relationships of a range of services with parents and families. 'Parents as Partners' may require more flexibility in interpretation if parents juggle multiple appointments, assessments and the balance between childcare and employment.

An American study of the child care practices of parents of young children with special needs (Booth & Kelly, 1998) found that lack of knowledge of the child care needs of children with disabilities or special needs was a significant barrier for parents seeking day care arrangements. The same study notes that most early intervention services are provided from a centre base and where the early education and intervention can be linked to child care arrangements, children will get the best service. However, the study remarks that such arrangements are not the norm. In practice many parents of young children with special needs have to use relatives.

Many EYDCPs are recognising that young children use individual carers such as relatives or childminders. Therefore 'parental involvement' and the achievement of the early learning goals will mean partnership with and training for whoever has care of a child at a particular time. Some are already working with childminders and other 'one-to-one' carers to ensure that they utilise the full range of early years provision in the area. Sure Start will hopefully give useful lessons on how individualised personal support, as well as more family-friendly services, will engage the traditionally 'hard-to-reach' parent in his/her child's education and development.

Conclusion

The range of new initiatives offer an unprecedented opportunity to improve the quality and coherence of early years services. The United Kingdom, like the USA and the majority of countries in Western Europe, is moving towards closer integration between education and childcare. Initiatives like Sure Start and Quality Protects also acknowledge the impact of social disadvantage, poor health and housing and parental vulnerability upon young children's well-being, education and 'life chances'. Within all these initiatives (and many others such as Health and Education Action Zones, the Healthy Schools Initiative and Health Improvement Plans) there is a real opportunity to achieve the 'joined up services' which successive Governments have advocated but seldom achieved. The advent of a Disability Rights Commission and Human Rights legislation will sharpen the debate about discrimination and education. But challenges will still remain. Sharing of 'best practice'; the accessibility of appropriate advice and support for the growing diversity of early years providers; good quality training to create services capable of meeting new standards for early years education and care will necessitate a strong national strategic direction. Many providers would welcome a national strategy to ensure that special educational needs and disability are better addressed within early years services.

As the Early Childhood Unit (1998) notes, good quality early years provision transcends the traditional child health, educational and social care divides. In effect it:

- creates a shared language for all Early Years Providers

- unifies and consolidates the strengths and skills of diverse approaches and settings

- extends practitioners' understanding of children's development and learning

and, in the case of children with disabilities or special educational needs, maximises their life chances and actively engages parents, families and communities in their ongoing development. The integration of early learning and child care will challenge everyone and at a time when 'best value' is a key policy objective, it also creates a powerful research agenda to guide policy, target resources and assess qualitatively as well as quantitatively what works for children, parents, professional care givers and educators (Nichole, 1998).

Evaluation of the current Government initiatives will be crucial, with active dissemination policies of effective policy and practice. Planning for disability and SEN within the new diversity of providers will be essential - as will the setting of clear targets within LEA Education Development Plans and the expectation that all early years services will have SEN Policies which can inform audit, review and inspection. But the framework is there.

But as Frank Dobson, speaking at the launch of 'Quality Protects', commented:

'Within the new range of Government initiatives, we have the unique opportunity to integrate the education, health and social care of all children in this country. If we can improve the "life chances" of these children, then we need earlier identification and intervention; we need to build up and build upon the capacities of families and support them in being good parents. We also need to raise competence and confidence in all providers - recognising that "excellence for all" is a corporate and achievable responsibility.'

References
[This list includes additional reading as well as sources for references given in the text]

Booth, C. and Kelly, J. (1998) 'Child-care Characteristics of Infants with and without Special Needs: Comparisons and Concerns', in *Early Childhood Research Quarterly,* Vol 13, Number 4, 603-623.

Child Psychotherapy Trust (1999) 'A Sure Start for children's lives?', in *The Child Psychotherapy Trust Review, 1999,* No 18, Summer Issue.

Council for Disabled Children (1999) Quality Protects: First Analysis of Management Action Plans with special reference to children with disabilities or special educational needs and families, Department of Health.

DfEE (1999a) *Early Years Development and Childcare Partnership: Planning Guidance 1999-2000*. DfEE Publications.

DfEE (1999b) *Good Practice in Childcare: Networks and Networking - A Guide for Providers of Childcare and Early Years Education*, DfEE Publications.

DfEE (1999c) *Good Practice for Early Years Development and Childcare Partnerships: Developing and Supporting High Quality Sustainable Childcare*, DfEE Publications.

DfEE (1999d) *Good Practice in Childcare: A Guide to Training and Development*, DfEE Publications.

DfEE (1998a) *Meeting Special Educational Needs: A Programme of Action*, DfEE Publications.

DfEE (1998b) *Meeting the Childcare Challenge*, DfEE Publications.

Department of Health (1999a) *Social Services Performance in 1998-99: The Personal Social Services Performance Assessment Framework*, Department of Health Publications.

Department of Health (1999b) *The Government's Objectives for Children's Social Services*, Department of Health Publications.

Department of Health (1999c) *Local Authority Circular (99) 33, Quality Protects Programme: Transforming Children's Services 2000-2001*.

Department of Health (1998) *Local Authority Circular LAC (98) 28: Quality Protects Programme - Transforming Children's Services*.

Dickins, M. and Denziloe, J. (1998) *All Together: How to Create Inclusive Services for Disabled Children and their Families*, National Early Years Network.

[The] Disability Rights Task Force (1999) *From Exclusion to Inclusion: A Report of the Disability Rights Task Force on Civil Rights for Disabled People*, Stationery Office: London.

Early Childhood Unit (1998) *Quality in Diversity in Early Learning: A Framework for Early Childhood Practitioners*, National Children's Bureau.

Kahn, J. and Russell, P. (1999) 'Consulting Children' in *Special!*, Summer issue 1999.

Mental Health Foundation (1997) *Don't Forget Us: Report of the Committee of Inquiry into Provision for Children with Learning Disability and Challenging Behaviour*, The Mental Health Foundation.

National Deaf Children's Society (1999) *Quality Standards in Education - England*, National Deaf Children's Society.

National Disability Council (1999) *Code of Practice on Part III of the Disability Discrimination Act 1995: Access to Goods and Services*, Stationery Office: London.

Nichole, Z. (1998) 'Welfare Families Use of Early Childhood Care and Education', *Early Childhood Research Quarterly, Volume 13, Number 4*, 567-571.

Parents at Work (1999) *Waving not Drowning*, Parents at Work Publications.

Pre-School Learning Alliance, Inclusion in Pre-School Support for Children with Special Needs and their Families, PLA publication.

QCA/DfEE (1999) *Early Learning Goals*, QCA Publications.

QCA (1999) *Early Years Education, Childcare and Playwork: A Framework of Nationally Accredited Qualifications*.

Quality Protects (1999) 'Education: Time for Action' and 'Caring for Disabled Children' in *Quality Protects Newsletter, Issue 3, November 99*, Department of Health.

Sure Start (1999) *Sure Start: a Guide for Second Wave Programme*, Sure Start Unit: DfEE.

Sure Start (1999) *Sure Start: A Guide for Trailblazers*, Sure Start Unit: DfEE.

Sure Start (1999) *Sure Start: Making a Difference for Children and Families*, Sure Start Unit: DfEE.

Chapter 4
Summary of discussion
BRAHM NORWICH and GEOFF LINDSAY

Discussion at the seminar was initially in small groups followed by the reporting of main points to the whole group which led to further general discussion. The presenters then responded briefly to the discussion. What follows is a summary of some of the main points which small groups reported back to the plenary and the final responses.

One group identified three themes: funding, multi-disciplinary work and training. There were some concerns about the sustainability of various initiatives, especially as funding depended on LEA matching central funds. There were also doubts about what was meant by multi-disciplinary work. There were suspicions across different cultures. Demographic factors affected the implementation of multi-disciplinary work, for example in rural and urban settings. As regards professional training there were questions about how to foster empowerment and get around the issue of professional isolation. There was a need to develop alternative models of support which went beyond a simple concept of outreach, e.g. one which involved the loaning of equipment.

Another group discussed what was involved in a model of 'trans-disciplinary' work. This was considered to be a higher level of collaboration than 'inter-disciplinary work'. It was considered to involve developing better understanding of how other professions worked in schools. It was thought that there was no alternative to finding ways of breaking down professional barriers. Questions were also asked about SEN involvement in Sure Start. Did the Sure Start model have a vision of practice on the ground? Experience in one LEA was of an existing support service being drawn into Sure Start. The need for organic developments raised questions of how this was to be achieved. The benefits of this were emphasised; widening the net of good practices and working with children at a much earlier age. Another point was about how the links between early years and SEN had a historical focus on disabilities and not on delayed development associated with poverty and socio-economic disadvantages. In talking about early years and SEN we needed to be clear about this history and to widen concepts to include issues concerned with delayed development. This group also had discussion about the use of qualitative and quantitative indicators in assessing personal and social development. Some identified contradictions in Government policy. There was a new emphasis in the National Curriculum framework on personal and social development, but assessment frameworks were still narrow. This led on to considering the question of target setting and what counted as a target. Some expressed the need for wider concepts of targets and standards with the suggestion that present models were over-technical.

The third group focused on the question of multi-disciplinary service delivery. The Portage model was favoured as its principles were relevant to effective service delivery. One person represented the range of professionals to the family. The programme of work was focused with there being regular contact and parents seen as part of the solution, not as the problem. The keyworker idea from this model was seen as important for professional training, especially for joint training. The significance of having a common language across professional groups was also emphasised (for example, to link concepts like 'disability', 'special educational needs' and 'in need'). There was also the need to have common key indicators across professional groups for when guidance and help was to be made available. Different professional groups could share their ways of passing on skills to parents. Monitoring outcomes was also important as professionals need to know when they have been successful. How to get resources to the point of need was another issue as there were often delays in doing this.

The fourth group discussed concerns about the forces which inhibit early years provision from providing for diversity. One of the main identified factors was the new regulations in minimum staffing levels. Another factor was whether the early years goals could be interpreted in relation to local settings and conditions. Another factor was the question of transport. Funding was also identified as a main issue in relation to the training needed for local provision which dealt with the generality of SEN. What was needed were clearer local policies.

The general discussion which followed ranged across various matters. One question was how early years issues would influence the revision of the SEN *Code of Practice*. What were going to be the criteria of need? More emphasis was required on developmental processes and on being able to evaluate responses to provision; to the impact of interventions. What was needed, some argued, was for greater focus on entitlements and not needs. With Sure Start it was felt that there was a chance to start with a fresh slate as this initiative was geared to looking beyond specific agencies. A tension was identified between individual resource seeking and the development of community processes and provision. How this was resolved would have an impact on the criteria of need in the revised SEN *Code of Practice*. Another issue was whether the early years goals would have an impact on pre-school funding and the issuing of Statements. Will there be teething problems?

Another strand of general discussion was the question of evidence-based aspects in relation to the use of objective/subjective criteria of need. It was argued that a concern for quality provision requires a concern for the qualitative aspects of the provision. Evidence-based also meant facing questions of how to evaluate the sharing of skills with parents and others. The general direction of the discussion was in favour of not only using quantitative but also qualitative indicators.

The nature of additionally resourced schools was also touched on. For some these are the antithesis of inclusion. It was noted that in the USA there is a move in some states to adopt this model of inclusion. The rationale was that it had the benefits of avoiding isolation, providing concentrated expertise, resources, and staff training but in a mainstream setting, thereby offering pupils a peer group. Some disability groups there were favouring this model. It was pointed out that this model did not mean a separate special unit, but a resourced school which enabled pupils not to feel isolated as the sole child with a particular kind of difficulty/disability. It was also noted that it was important to listen to the children as they will tell adults how they feel. The discussion led to renewed calls for working out what was meant by inclusion and how we recognise it in a way that related to Government policy.

What is involved in the 'early years' was also raised in general discussion. It was pointed out that the 0-3 years phase was different from the 3-5 years phase, a distinction that needed to be made when we talk about provision in the early years. This point was linked to the other question touched on in discussion - which children are we talking about in the relationship between early years and SEN?

Sheila Wolfendale in her brief final comments noted that diverse themes had come out of the discussion, such as the need to evolve a common language and how we know that we are successful in provision. The main themes were related in her view about the need to realign early years and SEN, parental partnership, training and evidence-related practice. She reminded participants of the model of a US child psychologist, Lilian Katz, who suggested that quality assurance was about finding out the views from above, from providers, from children, from parents, but also from posterity, how future generations would judge provision.

Philippa Russell picked out several themes from the discussions. One was the changing language and culture in this area of work, with SEN as a significant aspect. Other themes were partnership with parents and what counts as early years. The response of one London LEA to Sure Start was to enable a multi-disciplinary group of professionals and parents to project their preferred ideas and visions unaffected by criteria. A reshaping of the services was going on. There was also a need to feed these ideas on the early years phase into the revision of the SEN Code of Practice. Finally the debate about inclusion needed to continue. The US message was that taking account of parents' perspectives and responses was important.